Sunrise Poison

Sunrise Poison

Phillip Zhuwao

2018 © Deep South
ISBN: 978-0-9947104-2-0
ebook ISBN: 978-1-928476-28-3

Deep South
contact@deepsouth.co.za
www.deepsouth.co.za

Distributed in South Africa by
University of KwaZulu-Natal Press
www.ukznpress.co.za

Distributed worldwide by
African Books Collective
PO Box 721, Oxford, OX1 9EN, UK
www.africanbookscollective.com/publishers/deep-south

Some poems in this book have been published in *New Coin*, *Tripwire*, *Afro*,
Southern Rain Poetry, *Poetry International*, and *Other Voices Poetry*, and
anthologies *It All Begins: poems from postliberation South Africa* (2002)
and *State of the nation: contemporary Zimbabwean poetry* (2009).

Original text design: Paul Wessels
Revised design and layout: Liz Gowans
Cover design: Megan Ross

for

Josephine-Nyasha
(died 20 August 1993)

Why depart when I am writing my first gems, why the fire why such a departure? Can words mean anything then, can memorials bring such moments back again, songs are sung such moments are seen, God's plans take place; His Hand we only Praise.

Sneva J. Marengu

Only living grandmother left, those meals those days and those beautifuly-pleasant chidings that I tease you about, such moments!

Peter-Juma P.Z.

The DJ man, such uncontrollable binges, all the same thank you for the long welfare as we wait for the right day. Don't forget the days I called at the dreary reception. Greetings Father.

Emma-Mamvula

Huge meals made the Poet Inspiration and the Stings produced these for you to see for your relief your waiting and your painful calls as the patient-nurse, aint it beautiful mother.

CONTENTS

sunrise poison

awakening
and the
poems of shit

promises
and
shrapnel

the sunset poems

books betrayal
spray of shit

shrapnel!
fuck the laws in poetry

dates the disappearing act

Phillip Zhuwao 1971-1997

Sunrise Poison was completed in 1994, when Phillip Zhuwao was 23 years old. At the time of his death in January 1997, he was working on a second book of poems, and had completed two short novels.

Zhuwao's grandfather was originally a Lozi from Barotseland, while his mother's family came from Mozambique. This contributed to his family's disorientation: "I have three international identities, an abnormality hard to describe." (This quote and others come from bio-notes supplied by the poet).

His early life was full of hardship: "We had been evicted from many farms ... finally we settled at Chitungwiza, the urban centre of the tobacco farms. I spent most of my childhood in the tobacco, potato and cattle farms. Before I was to school, my uncle taught me Russian revolutionary history. It never interested me, but some names gave me inspiration." Phillip completed most of his school education at Chitungwiza. "I saw bullets and blood. My father was a soldier. In 1987, to try and forget the terror of Inkomo Barracks and the panga knives, we shifted to Kuwadzana in Harare."

His literary education was self-taught. "I read every book I came across, Shakespeare, Kipling, Rider Haggard. The books I couldn't buy I read in the bookshops, Kingstons mostly. I had to risk the wrath of security guards and the police. I would enter a bookshop, pick up *Don Quixote*, check for guards, and start reading where I left off the last time ... I read many books this way till I was unwelcome at the bookshop."

Zhuwao became fascinated by the Russian poets Pushkin, Mayakovsky, Pasternak, Akhmatova and

Tsvetaeva, as well as by classical greek mythology, and European modernists: Pound, Eliot, Joyce and Rilke. References to these writers are scattered through *Sunrise Poison*.

Despite his immersion in European literature and mythology, he remained grounded in African traditional culture. "Colonialists said a lot about African culture without understanding it. They mangled the little knowledge they had into horrendous tales of terrible witches and cannibals and shrieks of old hags sending chills down your spine. Rider Haggard was the most terrible. When Christianity came, it attacked loudly all African customs as devil-worship, refusing to get within, to understand and respect another man's comprehension of God."

Death and poetry were his abiding obsessions. "In 1987 death began to affect me personally. Dambudzo had died, my beloved cousin had died of haemophilia. Josephine Nyasha died after dousing herself with paraffin after a fight with her husband." Premonitions of his own death abound in *Sunrise Poison*. But, as he wrote in "my blue resignation conclude":

In their short lives
Poets live longer

Deep South will be publishing Phillip Zhuwao's complete works in four volumes, edited by Robert Berold and Alan Finlay. S*unrise Poison* is the first, and the only text to have been co-edited with the author. The second will be the prose work, the two novellas *See, the Barbarous Lands* and *Iron Fleece*.

– Robert Berold

inside out

tall dreams possess that short zest

Tall dreams possess that short zest
of energy that makes you run all night
In that dark 27 hours per day
When 11 pm rings at 7 o'clock
And
To turn the pillow doxypol fuddled
Knowing she's not there at all
Never!

But to dance the poem's anguish sentence rhythm
of devious pats you'll get back soon
You see I told you.
You've seen it.

Digging the Future's grave molten bones
Weeping the brass pages to rusty premonition –
Omen (Amen)
But why didn't you even tell this drip
These walls these crushing sympathies
I've
Seen these clocks tick
And watched love's calendars peel and ditch
Wearing this black now blue jersey of slavery
(Emily, is that the lid for that pot!?)

I've loved, I've wept and

I have slumped welcome's weariness
But why?

I have not seen it.

what love moons
over this doorway confused?

What pain rends the sky's shroud so dark

O long riva without ends (amends)
rift that repels forever and today
a broken beginning why postpone what we know
is nothing but timeless school to a fool

to periscope your many hearts and pick mine
scattered on the dinner plate of years to come
conquered by danger's fear I munch ma being
dancing in God's stoic penumbra
I've watched ma self
        ma pen (ma mother)
And criticized and talked to ma self
        again

        Why her?

The fool's question lingers on the lips of the shovel
To scoop out compost warmth of society's venoms
And then

Gee
It's fair
One is to 1

The radio from Naziweek magazine
fluttering like butterfly her pain of insults

beatnik hammerz the Hun

Definitely
is this the end?

the lovely whore!

The Poetry will Sleep under the bed
Who will write it (colour)
Fool, little love

A window feels to not go
And like poetry's incest to fester
Just kiss ink's greeting
tearing away

Smouldering cemetery flawas an'
        memorials
        scalding-palsy

Yorick's head – middle night.

the broken dollar in polana hotel

A midnight torpsy-turvy
building trembling
Over mortar negotiation
full swing party
And the naked smile.
Osagyefo.
A hand raised
from left to left
uhuru UHURU
Confused like a balcony
jumping from the ground
Listening is shit
over valley purchase,
hesitant Pekinese and Peking
Clenched tight tsk tsking
highlighting the necessary
Swiss holiday.
Ornating the Povo Spa droughts
Why should I bow
When your flag wrings
Smiling that cold smile,
Midnight
garroting New day's beginning.
(Love
but I wasn't there)

from nowhere suddenly dew

Names of whispers thru names
broken walls
deathly pale
No drums beat again.
rainbullet + scandal =
Doldrums
and hooks and falcon sharp beaks
over and round
her breath hissed coolly on my breast
to Scotchroast deep
it was morning already

night without pain

Manicured smiles flood on the Canvas
Savanna's thighs slither nowhere. Hiccup
of last morning's Spumante rivals
This huge clot on my helpless tongue
I've bled for days and walked for hours
till I saw God in his absence. mystery.

Haven't I listened to the music of time's end
recording and have done nothing but all

I write like madman times don't exist

In your sexual obituary when
your not not being there betrays, but attracts
the Cuba face of love during olympic Space
        grinning an olive skin
        and the heavy patter of rain
        on my heart
        Shattered phoenix

never to rise.

my blue resignation conclude

In their short lives
Poets live longer

Disabled tongues snap red
Smack lips red lisps blood
again

Causing shortsighted hiccups
talking
asking

Do I longer plead
O love

Farm after farm Squatter
Permanence
Why?

Tell me
Threnodies of threat only beginning
And end no middle of
this snapping
Wire sound of
spattering faeces

Raging moon blue bolts leap
roasting on the bones of my fire
We swallowed whole chunks
Of unpronounced vocabularies

To look forth back

        agasp
Lot's girl
freaked

I turned word with no Sense
Why spite yourself then
to me rot my heart in flames of rust

Curse of thirteen splash of flood's fountain
        genius

Cloud of dust fast rodeo on horizons
Cataclysm orgasm on Galatea's rigid
        She
        Turn
        turn!

And then when we meet
A thousand times no more
        Will you see me again?

The cherubic face contorted
of boil's Point

Pouting macho after macho
of tequila roasting penises
with assados of burning wire

Slightly around my Scrotum

We never Sing knew Song
but plot and press electric hot
irons over...

ode to god

...Whose children burn mercedes tyres
for heart warmth in Spring's Spite... the
words are beautiful promises
that fell thatches undone
for his hand, bane, smites
the man's words in the fields (forests)

To watch the horroizons swell
on my forehead this bee
busy with a fly, hope's omen
and
When Gods tumble in defeat
    What!

Chance to Afrika is man to hold tight

The moon drops two gourds
one with clean knives
the other poisonous kilts
to drape the Virgin Soils blowing
to the hectic desert winds

Lioness's roar whirlwind of the rivers
Shake the skyscraper of foul
On a single hill of clotting blood
to scatter, smithereens of Spirit's anger
and his Denial

Nothing is what it seems (looms)

We wrote many poems in the floods
And sought shelter in the leopard's claws
Nobody was hungry yet
Death lived to age and to young
to watch smiling
as
we cannibalised the ruins
of the history's time.

iron shit

Listen
Once you grow
that's just that
Are you not an adult?

This is the last meal on my place
Go there go where
Go mad I don't care
Take your pen
Your books
Your papers
And your shitty poems
Don't be there when I phone

The milkman sang
        how many pints.

The baker smiled
        the croissants or these.

On the lawn a marmalade jar
        spilt a red delicious and.

The man strode out
the suitcase under the arm
the smile a hesitant challenge
this is Monday
how time flies.

cain and abel

Tom-tomming the dark hills away
I remember
the crescendo dirged the not yet dead
and the nights, those long, long nights
shivered in slavery from Wraiths unappeased.
The Chanting Sorceress called
immediately the prophecy came true

out in the valleys
Blood began to flood
Cain and Abel.

sentiment's lane

The moon's shadow dances darkly.
The owl thinks of yesternight's rat.
And the blue stocking on image's mirror.
    Poetess, flicks the pages slowly
    mildew
    my lines tremble in the night: decapitated neons!

Switched by each other's memories
And those whispers a hararean maze of promises
daren't we talk of everything
of the flower in the broken jar
of pregnant bubonic distress
of Socrates' scabies
and the dream/night wore on

Behind gone's foggy trial
that shakes the miasma of melancholy
to inquire to the stretch
    does this lane turn?

from scratch
my love
from scratch

sycamore tree

dancer of the wind, what shouts
from your song? I see
London's sleet
and I retch.

To feel the sun and the terriers
then the slums and scabies
I think of Harare rare of warm nights

Hyde history
Piccadilly and so
Can I be bought!?

And here is the tree
Raining this rain
my brow is cold.
I won't be under here
next time

What a park!?

thinking

Blast the night!
Your death doesn't know!
You were calling my name
When you purse your lips
And I see the grass swaying
I say
"Is this the prayce"
Why do words do me nothing

i am her opened legs

Cavity swallowing voluptous flaming magma
I write on the blank pages of this book
Watching lilies flame out of my last poem
the sun has sunk half the houses ago
blood ebb out to urge me on to just
Yesterday's lovemaking

Her sofa has this broken leg
I have to be very careful
the jagged broken bottle waves on my crotch.
beads of fear drop pale the sunset

Am I going

payday looms there's no collection
but broken calabashes of tears' salt
plus stamps and charred nails.

my brain feels today's hunger

Are these words
Are these words I the outlaw
is my love really dying out there in London
is she a whore unwholesome in Amsterdam
will her plane beatnik in the ocean, kaput!
is I shoot her
I with the Radiant smile o' my Black
ravage IM GOING THERE AGAIN
thru walls anarchy anus

the days mingle again
the question begin again, hogwash!
the old womany stupid voice is not dead
remember
remember

I've never liked Diphthongs

How should we be one 2 difrent
Worms in the snow eating the snow –

the red/blue earth's palmistry

zigzags
like
a broke
n
sarcophagus
over horizons in mind's reading

... and love wept

Morning cloud has come
Will you be under its shade?
It's like I'm watching this city
Under an angel's siege
It's like I'm watching
Narcissus holding himself.

I've seen death's nobility over all
I've seen the incest of two cities
And I've sensed adultery's shudder
and the night's voice
darkly

"Where are you?"

But of this
I've seen nothing
But

I'll wait under morning cloud
and catch the descending tears
pretending they are hope's victory
over those sad truths
... and love wept.

bricks
magma
then
love

why should those big eyes not see?

The days have got no colour ie
they are not hazel but beautiful mounds
of meal of rotting worms
these I fail to touch are
her 2 breasts mound of grave meat

Crushing her nails amidst the tumbling bricks
She rises
Ashen gargoyle face we tangle
I am lo
and
She is lo

The oil between our thighs is
from pressed shit
The caresses we shit over and over
is crushed faeces

Why should we mean nothing to each
When we're really nothing.

timeworn

Timeworn is anger's age that scribbles
slowly of Death's Brain.
Sloughing, Sloughing, Ending.
But Phoenix, Resurrection.

Today Comes, Tomorrow Ends.
I loved you.
My hand aches.

Watch the calendars peel
And the seasons wilt
Newtime's Poet
Will dance dance's dance

I'll hold you
O.

I'm so sad.

When you paint your daybreak
I'll see your rising rays
Like daggers drawn, a challenge.
To whom, God, me.
Why?
Haunt's question.
T
    U
       R
         N
            a
            round

In the looking glass. It's you I see
Those eyes. A laughter's distate.

Your love is Time.
You don't know.
Hiss kiss is betrayal.
Timegone, he'll turn
And you'll turn to me.

Critical eye roves the plaintiff waltz
Pumice struck my cleanness
metamorphized to leprous
Society's ptomaine stomached my psalms
Incognito. God's clenched jaw grew cold
as the days pass stared back
The jacaranda's blood dripped like eve's partum.
I watched as Röntgen's laugh stopped smuck!
before my chest's coy smile rod

Struck dumb the darkness metathesis prowled
I
the writer was groping for myself
in the metre's miasma

As the crowd's leery grinding invited
my palsy shadowy attendance searched
Where?
Where?

is this a dream again?

We move along this road
how many years today. Today
we try to shame death
as she lies cold and still

over the bushes, in the dry grasses
three women walked, one in swimsuit brown
and we poke fun. Newsreader!
Then I talk like de Intellectual
and caress with no force

over undulating slopes,
the insatiable newsreader demands and drains
then I burst clitoris, red she sinks
    The rivers are pale pale blue
     to thin into fingures of sewage waters
      that choke in dead grasses and hyacinth
Her body sinks 'cept the head that remains still
as I go over two more voyeurs then to
feel
this
morning drain.

irene's iron pearls

She arches her back
As pearls of laughter's pain
pierce thru the ceiling
and rock my attic

She models on the bed
and does the war cry – montezuma
then smashes the mirror's wardrobe
jagging my image to the wind

She strikes the pose
and clutches her buttocks
and goes berserk on my pen
then howls like hippolytus
as I drive into her.

correction's error or
when the poisons fall

God's
Cold smile
Savagery teeth a shine a while
Rum and rhyme and drops hurrying done
Cruelty-embrace that gasps
a thousand millipedes in the fridge
in expressionless silence in the morning
on lawn to sheol's gardens.

Vignette against triple letters of treason
Nights of debts dry broken pencils

God's confetti burnt my eyeballs

her buttocks, mountainous torture
trembling, myriad of nakedness

There was no point

    She brought with her
    a torture's chamber
    full to the testicules
    clutching the kit

In the train was Alexander Dumas
eating popcorn head nodding
    nodding

In the moonlight's shadow

Why
?

thou has ravished my heart
my sister my bride

Two fawns, two hills of fern
A valley's tear the hand of
God's strike
has striken my woes loose

From a dance's dream, winter's warmth
I fear my love for you.

> what is love
> my fingers rove

And lick the hive's ambrosia
Why mutate me?

In dawn's clatter over hunger's denial
hunched small under the tarpaulin
of ennui Cackle
thrust aside by the first's cackle
of a winter blazed by arthritic bones

I saw rising
like a falling star

Princess, a ghost not yet dead
Where was my fillip's raucus mania?
The grasses sway in fate
from thence you leap and hurtle to fall
O
I won't recognise you everywhere
But on the fingertips of poem's index.

is there forgiveness in women?

Sorrow's farewell
When hoped for
jumps slowly away
to become this
"please"

Night's song of agony embrace
under the moon
two ghosts
is a sigh to hide
between this pages and gulps

To me it's over
The dance has ended
Its moon's farewell
"Where's my beginning?"

How many times?
does my eye shrink
when there's nothing to see
but your "NEVER."

sunrise poison

times are i'm afraid of this death

Ashes of nylon navels and shoes that are shrouds
of last smiles and formaldehyde

Again the point is
It does not matter whether you understand me or not

I listen to this womany talk
of being broke from payday to doomsday
and phoenix ashes in the winds scatter
last particles on my single mindindividual face

This woman is my (r)age, and I don't believe it!
She claps her hands like my mother
and I can't rise from my seat
The firewood isn't yet dry
and choking smoke enters nostril sepulchres
there's no law for death

I'll phone you, but strictly not tonight.

and now that hell is in love

Shuttering two walls together, Kidnap
Kidnap KIDNAP supper's yell all night
Having rescued the flower in the rubble
Then to rush

I mean rush

To jot the lines slowly
My sista's onanism with my tight strung shadow
Wakens the lion in my bowels
And this lip these white teeth
Shudder deliriously a cleopatra devour

Necrophilic bang bang bang
She shoot thru the heart's alas
And alas the corpse died again
to wiggle into turbulance's birth

We are all dead humans, said the madman
because we die life's death.

the din that is writing poetry

Over Mrs. God's clatter of saucepans chiding
Hiding behind burning cigar hopes
is this
Samora's coffin of struggles
Why pallbeared by perilous topography
Shit.

Damn damn damnation the rape of harare.
And 'polispreadeagled masturbating
a dancer's condom
In the End my heart becomes

Cyclop's empty head.
O Fuck!

the blossoms were (chinese art)

Moaning in the jagged jade of sunshine
Swinging the parasols of God's fingers
On Ezra Pound's bow the peach burst
And the Perfume of sex mingled in the grass
of dead maidens' dynasties.

When the rising sun of mind's glare shuttered
The bits scattered glowing on the arid hills
In the morning consolations
Human limbs swayed in hell's hallucinari
Over pain killer's exposed tongue
It rolled out imagery's art
Then ah
        It was Byron's cur Lion
        God to hear him over his friend's pyre
        The boiling sea filled harare's fountain
        And lion philosophised "Eureka",

        From my twin thumbs
        Twin bolts of blue flame's incense
        Spurt out in chinese grace...
        Too late, the body of the fire
        Smouldering, and Heine's
        Hair stood in Africa Unity Square.

And blood dribbled from the blossoms
(Love today it's not a wish).

the jar of chrysanthemums

Gold overwhelms that purple in the Sun,
Her shades on the table and
Breakfast's coy smile

"Have you slept well?"

letter of death

Flicker in the avalanche tumbles
undone mirror's fly obscenes tomorrow's
remembrances
This
Country music's flail
leap on the malawi lake fishes
to see red fire flowers your story to me
Sitting under your feet the mud brightens
harare's ignorance and sugary liquid spilled
from my lips to my listening
Why the big fowl was the talk
Inheritance the tarmac LOMAGUNDI
black sweet from time gone
I was not there forgive me not
In white the woman between fire's vista
Signal. They danced for you how many times
The real dances stop forever my friend
In the paddocks of my imagination eery
fodder flame from opened palms
smothered by green Mulanje's silence
the words quietened in the breezes
and
the dirges realised the fake
of it
As we imigrants plot our histories
and conceal the jade sandal (please)
Under the planet of hearsay.

maenadis

With Gerac's gold clutched tight. On moon's lichen
Red fanged vampirella marriage
She spread her legs
    and laughed

In the hyena's feast.
    battlefield
    please thrust in
    kill me

Her heart on my heart's grasp
She spilled over
    URSUPER!
    REIGN!

As the vales shook crimson
(THE QUESTION THE QUESTION)

Why do I always weep over you?

trying to drink and write

Those chrysanthemums
the madam's shout over hoe's delve
It was the same
The same.

And Aida moved away
buttocks swaying.

on arguing

Down Football Avenue. Myriad legs
They kicked me
Her dream of mangle

Aida
(The door is open).

the rotten fruit

When was it?
When hunger's question pleaded,
"Can I?"

When was it?
When profit's smile drove the nail
"Times have changed please pay."

Is something dead?
Somewhere something is smelling
I hope it's not the fruit.

When man prays to God
and gets nothing
he gives nothing to his fellow man
For he will feel betrayed.

awakening
and the
poems of shit

siesta

between rose vista of laughter's swaying
two goddesses fight to the bible bile
I
yesteryear cess thinker
scrambled eggs dreg goo
thinking

Twang twang twang

trembles

trembles
it gushes the longing's pain pleasure ash
violently
dead before my death – you ask
Where were you?

I've stopped on this tablet
And gazed into my eyes
to painfully see the stoic of this town
Crumble on my shoulders and knees.

This is bad
Along the tarmac
Along corridors of darkness, today
forever
a blank verse in freedom's thinking.

when thought remains

Between us this wall thickens
and
Promise's whisper is silenced
Where can we hear
The laughs of innocence
and
The trusty pats on shoulders?
We remain
one two islands
bridged by this water
to become
dots from heaven's Sight
Two gulls' droppings.

always, i've loved big cars (6 july 1993)

Winter trudge, cycle's promise, no words as well
but parliamentary speeches
then sirens, the coldness
of the jerseyless knocking,

It seems
I've got no time for love.
No beauty riddles the chapped big smile,
I don't like this!

Treasures of byzantine, that scurrying in the hair
haven't I brushed these black walls?
Winter to cruel winter
and
this seepage in my blood
        Autumn's sloppy coffee

This skin touches glow
coaches stop and collect
I
Castaway to nowhere
Stand in God's drizzle,

Stopping is also paradox
I write, and the fingers crack

over tyre onslaught – gone

Sprawled on the lawn – no words again
Strong vomit of blood, of formaldehyde –

Why?
I will always love you.
– And I am surprised?

this morning nigger

The days have been like this
these past 4 days

I've been trying to sell
my 2 copies of New Coin for few coins
Veldfire ravage evicts
mice hares locusts and her beauty to the hunter
to believe
I've walked to town and back
to try and secure that University scholarship

It's vain and vulnerable
achille's heel my roofs crush me
over the hills the beautiful Vumba mountains
the grassy drakensberg the sand-particled kalahari
my biological homeland Barotseland
Lewanika's eye and my true identity

My heart is now a bomb
the dish of water that pilate washed hands

Indians smoke peace pipe
When I'm reading Oom Smuts' autobiography

We can sit in this sun
or beneath it

God's footstools
So long as
I have a single beer

When she crossed her legs on Farewell
She mentioned Upsaala Heidelberg
Then british airways. She was gone.

Baring the wolf's ivory fangs
trying to blaspheme if God slept at all
Wondering why poetry is personal
Why Im not yet dead the cat's whisker twitched
SHIT!
Again the blood and snot clotted in my nostrils
to the shouting outside

this dark little room where
the unmattresed bed
the tens and tens of books
the oversized jacket behind the door
the holed shoes
are POETRY themselves.

the rose with marigold blooms

Come
To see my grave I've lived on talk
Future is my death, my image
I've not died yet
I've died a thousand times
And
I've watched you die before your death
Over
Cordelia's brow Cleopatra's asp hovers
And
I hide between her thighs of anxiety
The
Uzi has shattered all fingers of art's fillip
And
Uncaressed moment's tree tumble
Watching
Summer's winter crackling behind Wenceslas' steps
Over
Epic over creased foreheads of wandering thoughts
Mocking
Nemesis' blindness gives eyes to Homer
Hello
Suddenly bouquets drop blood
Why?
Your watch in my heart's song everything
Generosity love hunger cruelty race
And then
Stop Press!
Today's awake yesternight rubs the eyes
Of Slogan's betrayal

Why weren't you here?
Scandalous
I watch your bloom
blue
The dance begins in the water
Afrodite
I had watched your tears
Yellow
It was the curtain of secret spy stories
Then
Red of virginity torn and blood's smile
With everything in between void
Potholes in flickering snake tongues
Adam and Eve
The bard jumped from feminist asbestos roof
It was asparagus on the table of her chest
Suddenly her Etna breasts rumbled and heaved –

The watchman shifted his weight of Principles
"Aha,
it's you again."

love with the cruel woman

Thorns of steel tears grasp desert leaves
Scanty of aftermath never to ask
But to collect excrement of stars rivalling
no one only it is moments
for remembrances that will never be there
but scorn of penetration wringing bliss
of scarlet blood talks and whispers
touching walls with breasts and waking
finding absence and makarovs and handcuffs.

the whiskers of art's sanity

A living monument on the plinth
of timegrey hair shakes the tresses of
an old child, Art.

Time.
Frustration
Capital letters,
Sweet words to Ophelia's child.
Requiem greetings between
Introduction and Cleopatra's looking glass
Only the broken mosaic river scampers
like an insane hare nowhere

watching the funeral
thru a cracked wall

The afternoon is wreathed in black sunlight
The page's dirge flutters like wings in a tomb
and then
back to reality

VIOLENCE!

Township aphrodisiac
A tear's mathematics
over Joyce's dignam
        poor paddy
        someone's daddy

Over shoulders of electric pylons
death's owl hoots in fear

and from the rear,
that was the doves drop
O
Spirit
a willow on the shiver.

promises
and
shrapnel

i drink the halitosis of last year's wines

MoonGold
Spat after spat label
stuck on my burning indifference
And God's pieces of song flung far and wide
Meaningless shrapnel and confetti
Those bawdy lovely songs great warm nights
And lonely arrival mocks my eviction
Around small fires of acacia pinpricks
Then her
Soft thighs glistening
tea and wooden corks
no names there but identity's incest
and olfactory heavenly greetings
to relish.

you drink the beer

And I get the drunkenness
We go to the de-lousing chamber
You snatch my dream man

I pat your shoulder brother
you your shadow smirks

In the cauldron in furnace
In the molten ore
In the scabrous poem

I begged in Afrika's bounty.

it

It polishes my shoes heavily
with the pubic of yesteryear's rape
and I
bits of the rat's hair
monuments money's hiccup
to calendar the raid's woes
slowly
before time's end
and mince
the pasts gone
on farm mire elephant grass
that seriously walk down moffat street
heaving shut up the rejuvenating wisdom
chateau swirl to laugh hysterically
reciting
   "Fount to Bachsarai"
Watching the rat spit in my eye
O Pushkin!

i want out!

the dancer is you in the Savanna rains
When you ask the bus to go on forever
and
the looking glass is you when
        definitely
Yu ask my buttocks of images in paraffin
roaring burning black in haephestus' furnace
the days are calabashes of dead palm wine
that blossom into red blood in the black ambulance
yu say your life is my presence
turned into destitute vocabulary

but I forget
Joan of Arc was White
Very White the paper of hell's menus blistered
and scalded my Steve Biko fingertips
When I looked back
the wayward bus was right in front of me
Its single tyre Cyclops' smarting eye

When they began talking of digris
She looked at me at my empty silence
        but you write write poems
        how come you got no degrees?

the stamps in this detention mind
turn livid like a charon capsizing in Urine
the smudges on my face are debating faeces
the wormz these my fingers are typewriter keys
the Cry in the raining nyt trying

trying
to mangle the english sanguage
I forget
my dreadline is close
I have taken my poems
I'll get the books when I
bring your money
the typewriter was neva mine

When this becomes so real
and the poem refuses to end
enslaving to write all hours
I know longer have tears to cry
remember
when I insisted on paying the bill
and yu knew I had no monies
and stared as I ate piles and miles of
spaghetti bread yu didnt know
that was my first meal in 4 days I
never said fasting was voluntary
Out the Savanna music kinged
        for appearance's sake
        let's hold hands

between pages of blazing gasps
your thighs when they crush me are delirium
bantustans
and the flags
words from Senghor silences the Wind!

The Winter moon imprisons girls
        poetessez with thighs like akhmatova
        and

!
blood red blobs drop on this poem
I'm not trying to emphaSIZE!
the blooddrops in my plate
Scarlet a red soup of gritty tears
gravel of brain sawdust
on the drill of time(s)
answer
What race was scipio africanus

the rains in the Savanna dance you
definitely.

like

Like a fight in my dream
And my demand
"Who gave you the permission"

Like a sweet song in the marshes
And my strumming
"I'm sinking"

Is you in today's thoughts
a scent in the orange garden
that rises in that quietness
to humour all the slaves

but

To wake sometime
Fire's reign a raze
and the head's slow shake

It's over
Eloi. Eloi. Lama sabachtani.

jezebel's bedroom

Like watching the vineyard in dew
From a king's hill to swoop down
and fall fall fall to pleasure's hell
this is it

I saw the anger's tremble
And the shaking finger
I lusted after that wrath
God
Why is the night so short

Bear me this letter
tell of the view please,
from this bed.

I saw this
And I smashed the goblet
I saw harare
I saw babylon
I lusted after it.

Please get the garden
You're king.

babylon in love

The lion stalks
The salmon leaps the stream
The phallus rears
REARS like anger's bellow
Babylon is in love

My queen my murderer this killer
I'll be Van Gogh
Castrate me this pain
And I'll dance in my blood
You'll eat my sin's chuckle

Dear Gomorrah
This is your love
    Sodom

Look!
Those concrete fields
I give you
Onyx-minded Beelzebub.

the sunset poems

unicorn at zim b awe loins

Don't talk of another time
Ignore the smoke of my spent fuels

Griphon upon Griphon upon granite map
My misfortune is

I'm too aware, too conscious;
Be patient!

I'm tearing up this vaudeville
height over height droning
chainsawing my neck

Gathering dust, bright dust
        her whiplash tongue
Mangle and mongrel breed to twist
        slowly my anguish
Really cry beautiful promises ever
        fire on fairy

death-me, see, fingers lotioning eye's picture
turning into a claw pulling useless workshops
and half chewed hearts
        dancer on bullet point
        pantihose provocation

My sister, many worlds in nowhere

        sometimes

I can't cunt explain my poetry
being there, time painstaking
hurrying all that beautiful night
Clutching today's answer
        today's night's stolen shirt

Has there ever been a question
building building builder
        Caution

I was never a budding Writer! Damn!

long nights endless, closed doors
Cold in the winter, drying paints

then What?

On the pubic spent catridges
Shorn in the splinting sunshine

Roads to Chitungwiza

Kalashnikov in black Highfield
Horseback paleface at Inkomo

        (W)RAPED IN THE POEMS of Kuwadzana

Lomagundi's strip blackened
never from the horizon

As dragon bearing semen splushed into what
was mine but belonged to God

to His pots cooking my pasts

Farm, mystique from a granite kopje
grasping a bobjaan's crooked tail
From baas' sjambok smile

Smile.

worms of steel

Back bending and youth seeing on treetops
Bridge over River Kwai why unfinished nothing
Caressing same song of death and defeat
Knuckles of cement shoving bayonets
of plots and gasps in the darkness of bygone streets

Knowing knowing

of nightmaric satisfaction
of high schoolgirl moving fingers
on the twilight beaches of barbed wire betrayal.

harare

a fallacy of God's dirty soil
low and high
Rising a haze of brown life without destiny
July August September
October will come, will it rain?
A homogeneity of crafts rafts bon voyage to doom
With devils aboard seeking the sea. Here?

hush hush (harsh) my love

It's
When I'm alive that
I'm afraid of Deth
(don't forget)
    the sand's blackmail
    the
    Ostrich's head in battle

they are many writers by the fireside
When pine logs crackled
forebodings of the dark's shadows

the 2 of us know
I won't stop you crying
no blood can fertilize colonised soils
deth is deth heroes burn in hell

longtime back we cannot
mention legends and executioners
Who said
    Poetry should not be corrected

this ocean mingles with the orange river

Cirrhosis blinds my eyes
but
the
muse
bids me stand on hill top –
    the grasses are vales Savanna dew
    my black brotha discriminates me

When bullocks fight
and Io is between those horns
what chance do I have

I like every man –
Jew or gentile
love
You know me thru and thro
was I politik those nights

Madness of me Cruel
I seem to talk to you
as if you smile before me

are crystallnachts these lullabies
that premonition granny's pregnancy

I've packed my bags every hour
yet my destination
seems
not to know me

On the doorway (hush
We are 2 lonely strangers (hush
Is the eagle decided to land (harsh

We no longer contemplate
I here
Yu there
as this continent
becomes a doormat
where angels make violent love
anointed by my blood...

sunset

Red of Time to sit all days
Still in the ruby silence and sigh

Then slowly watch the fractured marigolds
and sigh "It's not sentiment."

To watch the geese fly
and one behind straggling, ME.

Then say to the sinking sun
You are death for you don't die

And to think of Mozambique's shores
and the liners and the gulls.

And then harare, flowers cars
Women and the hospital drips.

Agh, to jump away from running lizards
realising Time doesn't mate, Agh.

Then dream as the sun sinks
of love's shudder in the mirror.

And then slowly, slowly
to rub the poem away.

books betrayal
spray of shit

the dunces at the helm

Elijah's ashes blew in the eyes
of the Poem's broken teeth mouth
Kuwadzana's sea blooms a black red
over the cockroaches of time
Redferns of a bygone bloom again
from my heart's whirlwind
Blowing the willows my entrance
In the offices of fame
O shame

What hero drove this chariot in the fable
and did his antics over my lines.

new generation poet

On someone's head the dreads only
gives me remind of you disembarking
To that avenue's flat I to nowhere
but to hospital irony call no goodbye
winged the flight your education
breaks the sands between us into no happiness

Light the paraffin lamp scrawls on roof
of night's loneliness once to scrub garlands
of thorns to scale passions of poison into
poison

to curse
maim to aim
rape disfigure
        paedophile

drake on she-goat
        angel on devil
        task
        shit
        hapless

pen dripping last year's Christmas turkey blood
Oslo
Tomorrow
Natal skirmish skin-head racism-Boche
        Dingaan

pieces of love

Nonsense
Bohlinger
Guiness
ejaculation   Marechera hang-over

cannabis
LSD
    methylated spirits

Faces smeared
with the madman's semen and saliva

for once, look the other way

I've slept on this floor
I've seen them feigning understanding
those looks!

My heart in a hot shrapnel
the whip rang in the morning radio
thru this grey wall
ink congested my nostrils' voice crying
thru the toilet window to
the aromatic heaven kitchen

Do angels thrive on manna and caviar
they thrive on maniacs like me
Who'd no chance to thrive decently

blue like hot ink the waters turbulant
like semen in her veins in her brain
Why?
I've never liked loud women because
Why should we be dancers
to heaven's look
        where are our poems!?

Scandal
the goldsmith's murmur rose

darling
darling
I'm trying to understand you this
the dates do not matter

I'm trying not to make you cry
my situation is just another judgement

flamingo buzzard flap flapped
to Zinaida Volkonskaya's salon
in the tavern
closing hour struck
Why are the streets so cold and empty?

shrapnel!
fuck the laws in poetry

mayakovsky

Is that Vassilisa
Hanging on the pylon
my
How the snow is deep today
Poor girl
How ugly she's turned

left at the Crimea
is this widow's love
that I see today
as the gun's spittle

The poet spoke
of Akhmatova's moving lips
Rasputin, naked
diving in the deep snow.

the microwave

Lunch's welcome lingered
electricity wafted from the kitchen
and he shook his head at me.

You will have to lunch out.
She's phoned the technicians
The blasted microwave's dithering again
Sorry don't be so downcast.
Remember this house is yours

Out
in the blinding sun,
The child's lip trembled
as she clutched tearfully
mama's wilting valentines.

God!
He said the house was mine.

there are no beautiful policewomen

His pretty black smoke over sky blue slates
Paint the word Mother
On town's groin high heel deep

Anger
Bookseller's closure
mixes with the dead locked eviction
a scratch on the buttock with
the trigger of yesterwar's condolences
"Who's gone on holiday?"

Ambience of iron thorns to kraal
escaping blood to die a little
over D.H. Lawrence's nod in a beer hall
Striking challenges amidst beery gales

were they dreams

Moving like your whimperings
Scattered like broken mountains

Mounds your cries accumulate
to dance like shards of absent prisms

In the flowers of fires – your eyes
Writing in the sky – a dream

I saw you
Ithaca shuddered
     NO!

The fist of time opened
blood's bliss pouted – his burning moustache

Don't copy this, move to the other side

Mama
        ma
            ma
               (do
                   it softly)

It's his head in the cocktail
his head on the platter on the lawn
    before
    Herodotus

Messing myriads of her sinks

Mayakovsky!
I never shook your silver spools of hair
Blood bloodied shot on the snows

T'was her, banned again
    why

Her, the poem booked
fluttered mildew

is that ink

Is that mink in the cage of ice

Parallels to Riga Bucharest
    Cairo
    Downing Street

holding my chests
Into parallels of splintering bones and pencil ribs.

dates the disappearing act

another death, august 1993

Her smiles songs of beautiful weddings
blue moon colour of burning fire
Sleep and sleep
this book I'm writing
Such death can we wait another day

Stopping a week gone
She's really gone
        and down the soil piles

Tossing soil are flowers of dirt, Farewell
As we return one minus along the roads to this room

Calm and washing hands before the meal

dare we diminish to dusty disappearing

over horizons of vapour tears.

On the sole of your shoes (child of
the rose) behind your mottled picture
In the decanter of bane of whisky

Dostoyevsky withers on the tablet
of lonely nights agog with passions

She mingles in me in her – this city
We see deserts of sand
We see Zambia's soccer players dead
Barotseland warns me as ink's bloodbullets

drift towards maputo bastardry

When the lifts opened

    You couldn't write NEVER!

nude sunbath (white woman)

for wallace stevens

Flank signature of alabaster poesy
Shuffle groin of sand of holiday
of moon's colour Eve gone to town
Can I
Incest finger of pointing
footing blunt fronted shoes
Beneath glasses of spite mildew newspaper
And the talk
Sumptous shoulders my sister I'm dead
black skin wrapped by tears
     late

Beans, eyes, looks on heart's
hard tongue to devour
...wait
bell boy hope gaze to 10cm dollar
broken by sun shades tan
to warm food bye bye.

Printed in the United States
By Bookmasters